"Dan Provost's *Darting In and Out*, starts with a poignant, short poem for the late poet, Glen Still, whose words, Provost reminds us, are never really gone, leaving a lasting impression on readers and peers. The same can be said of Provost's work, as he takes the reader on a journey through dead highways and a paradise lost, offering honest words, an acute longing for love, and stories of the underdog. The political toadies of the day are swept aside with a devastating humor. There is a great sadness, but also of beauty, as Dan darts in and out of Massachusetts Hospital, and we are reminded that his pain is our pain, both as readers and fellow human beings."

-Luis Cuauhtemoc Berriozabel, author of
Make the Water Laugh

"This collection of poems by Dan Provost is a message inside of a bottle, left on the side of the road, and addressed sincerely to the lonely and damp. Climbing right into the depths and pulls up a sleeping bag to crack open a beer with those who have yet to find their way out. Reflecting upon the violent internal tendencies inside us all. He Describes the harsh shoulder turn given to those who find it hard to adjust to an even harsher reality. Using humor and the occasional lyrical wink to brighten up the mud and dismay. Often utilizing natures mystery and wonder as a catalyst for a perspective lens."

-Mac Thorn, *Fate of a Mullet*

"I've been reading Dan Provost for a long time. And every time I pick up one of his latest I'm reminded of the guy behind the keys, beneath the pen, the struggles and successes of what it means to be good at this life. What it means to be a good writer. That Dan is still out there doing it, getting down the word, plucking at guitar strings like truth in the dark makes me smile, and makes me want to try just a little bit harder at everything I do. Another fine collection of his "things." Don't miss it."

> -J. Lester Allen, *Beyond the Wounded Horizon*
> (co-authored with James Duncan)

"I see it all the time; I am sure that you do too, people who stop and seek shelter from the storm because they cannot see what dangerous situation may lie in waiting. They play it safe and stop, shaking their heads at the others who keep the accelerator pinned to the floorboard and travel right through, regardless of the outcome. Trust me, in this collection of poems, Dan Provost seeks no overpass to park under for safety. He pushes on, *Darting In and Out,* full speed ahead writing in a manner that is not reckless, but rather forehanded, as he navigates the highs and lows of love, the memories of a boy that grew into the man he now sees in every mirror, and the erratic rhythm made by the pulse of society. Dan seeks no shelter because he knows, like so many other writers know, that sometimes you just have to hit a storm head-on with forward momentum and push through it to reach the sunshine's open arms waiting for you on the other side."

> -Victor Clevenger, author of *Disordered Portion*

Darting In and Out

Poems By Dan Provost

Kung Fu Treachery Press
Rancho Cucamonga, CA

Copyright© Dan Provost, 2021
First Edition: 1 3 5 7 9 10 8 6 4 2
ISBN: 978-1-952411-61-8
LCCN: 2021936656

Cover art: *Sword and Dagger Fight* by John Petite,
Courtesy of the Glasgow Museums Resource Center
Author photo: Boston Globe
All rights reserved. No part of this publication may be
reproduced or transmitted in any form or by any means,
electronic or mechanical, including photocopying,
recording or by info retrieval system, without prior
written permission from the author.

The author would like to thank the editors of the following publications where some of these poems originally appeared:

"Midwife of the Blues" was originally published by *Spillwords,*
"Dystopian Nothing" was originally published by *Lothlorian,*
"Before the Fall," "Thesis Project," "86'ed" were originally
 published by the *Rye Whiskey Review,*
"Danny Boy and the Stone Temple Pilots" was originally
 published by *Heroin Love Songs,*
"Cheryl Galley" was originally published by *Flashes of
 Brilliance,*
"Imaginary Ideas with Everette" was originally published by
 the *Black Shamrock,*
"Going to Look for the Big Time" was originally published in
 Detritus,
"Stoned at Fenway" was originally published by *Punk Noir Press,*
"Fake News Letterman List… Ten Jobs Donny Trump Can
 Apply for After he Leaves the Oval Office" was originally
 published in *Winedrunk Sidewalk,*
"Simple as That" was originally Published by *Bold Monkey,*
"The Place" was originally published by *Deuce Coup,*
"Searching for Real" was originally published by *Drinkers Only,*
"Mike Webster" was originally published by *the Dope Fiend
 Daily,*
"Waiting for the Cardiologist" and "Trying Nature Out" were
published in *Medusa's Kitchen.*

TABLE OF CONTENTS

Untitled / 1

Midwife of the Blues / 2

Failed Again / 3

Purgatory Chasm / 5

Stroll with Spirit / 6

Jealous / 7

Dystopian Nothing / 8

Easy / 10

New Yearly Ritual / 11

Whores at the Capital / 13

Empty Threat / 14

Before the Fall / 15

A Toadie is a Toadie / 18

Cycle / 19

Danny Boy and the Stone Temple Pilots / 22

Arranged / 24

Cheryl Galley / 25

Freshman Year in College / 28

Imaginary Ideas with Everette / 29

Wellbutrin Blues / 31

Behind Blood-Shot Eyes / 32

I Love That Song / 33

Going to Look for the Big Time / 34

Stoned at Fenway / 36

Mourning / 38

Two Lives in an Instant (Why I am
   a Moral Pussy) / 39

The Quiet Demeanor / 41

Fake News Letterman List... Ten Jobs
   Donny Trump Can Apply for After he
   Leaves the Oval Office / 43

Thesis Project / 44

Simple as That / 45

Family Tree / 46

The Place / 47

God Helps Those Who Help Themselves / 48

Misanthropic Suburb Wanderer / 49

Out of the Loop / 51

After Reading Her / 52

Searching for Real / 54

Mike Webster / 56

Give Up / 58

Way Too Late / 59

Not Me / 60

Detachment / 61

86'ed / 62

Confessions of Mourning / 64

Waiting for the Cardiologist / 67

Trying Nature Out / 68

Pure and Hard / 70

Never Could Figure Out / 71

Look, see, think—wrap visions up in dirty iconic fashion.
Dart there, then here—finally
someplace,

where blood is pouring out of every dilapidated pore.

As always, dedicated to my beautiful wife, Laura and our dog--Bella.
Also dedicated to my godchild, Jennah Carlson...who deserves a better Uncle than me.

Untitled

for Glenn Still

The speed of
shock when the words
are gone--
Only rival a sadness when
true soul has died.

Midwife of the Blues

Chaos was
a bluesman's
shanty---

Disarray, with the
woman throwing
rocks at his voodoo
heathen ass.

The chords of
an acoustic guitar
echo from a bullwhip evening.

Failed Again

An honest measure
of my worth is
scribbled on dead highways.

Notebook paper,

tossed out of cars
like found fries entrenched in the seats.

One thought led to
another, some
semblance of a unified
phrase.

The beginning of a poem.

Then-- nothing.

Failed adjectives, failed metaphors.

All regurgitated…
Stolen…

Words colored in crayon.

Attempted, tried, observed.

jotted, erased,

denied, rejected.

Seen by maybe five or ten
searchers who also

looked for faith
once.

Ending as dime store
short spurts.
Tasseled in the winter winds…

Groaning within a hand
or
a face.

Purgatory Chasm

The chatter.
The questions.
The liars.
The pacifiers.

Who try to fill
my head with theories,
"ism's,'" reasons to
keep hating,
or find loving.

All beleaguered pain
confined within
one blank stare
out my window…

So, who do you
consider self?

Today?

Stroll with Spirit

The bootstraps
were loose

as I walked—

Forgot my way home.

Fell to the ground—
prayed, then
died—

Truthfully,
        I just want to be
        remembered.

Jealous

They toast their poetry
prowess with friendly
pushcart prize nominations.

While the true heroes
keep plugging away
on dusty keyboards…

Knowing that the meat
on the bone is only
tasty when you made
the kill.

Dystopian Nothing

Any small town.

Where the locals
see the white light

slowly diminish.

Their trump/pence
signs blowing in
the breeze…

Give you the stare
as you drive by…

Hardened, threatening
glare… gathered in
a group of calloused faces
and torched temper…

Ready to pounce on
the outsiders…

Stained America,
prepared to fight, shoot,
fire-- when the order
is given

by a cheap walrus,

in an oversized
suit.

We bleed little
sanity when the verdict is
announced.

Death and isolation will
come quickly…

Menacing men
will then pat other menacing
men on the back…

putting their rifles away

drinking a Budweiser
and giving the Hitler salute,

proud caucasian…

will win the stage,
carrying the bodies

to the next
holocaust

flames seen and celebrated
all along the
countryside…

Easy

Just looking at the snow
laden mountains out a filthy
window…

Seeing the morality of parents
holding their child's hand…

Escorted to the plumbing van or
the driveway plow.

Scooting inside with laughter.

Covid school over for today…

I am not noticed.
I am not seen.

Sight and isolation play
the part
of
who we
are and
who we aren't.

New Yearly Ritual

Roll up into
defenseless position
after the death
of your parents.

Ruin family get-togethers with
sober reflected face.

No comment
while the gossip spews
between brothers and sisters.

Tramp through February-June
in a drunken stupor, rely on
well versed quotes that
put a damper on mankind.

Resume fetal through July-October,
only acknowledge the urge
to self-harm.

Blow off Thanksgiving this year…
Blow off Christmas this year…

Retreat to pitch black
apartment…

Even noontime has accepted
your request...

Of early night.

Originally Published in my book One of the Crowd
Always Bleeds

Whores at the Capital

And the revival
that never took place.

That long line of hate
mongers, self-promoting
stingrays—

The breeze from
the dirty
almighty.

Still sings to
the beat of sauerkraut
effigies…

Those absurd
animals…

Who attack,
retreat

then cry,
make excuses,

when caught by
survivors.

Empty Threat

I shall say nothing until the time
comes again to be a man.

When that moment arrives,
I'll be here--

A cactus for a mouth.

Falling down intoxicated.

Mumbling vulgar threats
to the scamps
drinking Woonsocket Wine.

Before the Fall

--Then,
become angry about all the emotional
investment put into that *last
relationship*—cut the blinders off as you
find a bar open on the seacoast in January…

Where you go when silent mourning
is never questioned.

--Then,
sit on the cranky stool,
look at all the fishing gear and
pictures of striped bass being caught
by summer heroes, lauding their
weekend warrior victories.

--Then,
look around for a juke box, careful
not to relive her Aretha Franklin songs.
Music can be so evil sometimes.

--Then,
eye the barmaid—You and her being the
only two in the place. Her eyes taut, her
body tight from some exercise regime
to fight age.

But you can see the life wear in her
demeanor, the bored situation routine
given as you order a beer and a shot of
the bird.

--Then,
order another Miller Lite and whiskey, keeping
the suggestion open that you and she could
become something special—Try portraying
a sensitive man, who is worthy of being
loved…

--Then,
forget that thought when she slowly shuffles down the bar
and fills the shot glass…You look up, giving a smile and a
proper hello…She grunts, grudgingly responding, then goes back to
her Clive Cussler book.

--Then,
mentally encounter
every bartender
you fell in love with while
escaping the scraps of other
Ms. Finals.

--Then,
take your shot, gulp down
the beer—and leave,
without acknowledging her
existence.

--Then,
walk along the beach, shiver as the cold hits
the Wild Turkey brain,
arrange some
rocks with your foot, forming an abstract
statue in honor
>
> of
>
> > the lonely...

--Then,
dream that every anguish of your
pain is akin to the Who's *Sea
and Sand* video, visualize yourself
as that disillusioned kid, taking
the uppers and wishing the ocean would
decide the fate of suicide

for you...

--Then,
fall down, the breeze offers little
atonement with the broken...

--Then,
understand there ain't much in
this world that has not already been
suffered...Find no comfort in this thought...

--Finally,
Live sparse, die... definition
diseased...near the shore where everything
is equal...but no one really
cares.

A Toadie is a Toadie

Grover Dill, the toadie
of Scut Farkus in *A
Christmas Story.*

Mike Pence, the asshole
with a fly on his head.

Look hard if you want.

There really is no difference.

Cycle

A father's dream
for his son ends
in bored static.

The stale movement
of those who got stuck
in the factory

happens again and there
is nothing Daddy can do…

He swore he would never
be stagnant.

Joining the service.
Seeing the world.

Seeing death
at his feet.

In his hair…

Promised himself that
his kid would not be
witness to slaughter.

Coming home from
the carnage—begging
for the dream, pledged
to those who work, fight, and
put their hand on their heart

when the flag is raised.

Scarce opportunity however for
Dad… No degree, no plan after discharge.

He leaned into
the only place he knew…

The midnight shift at the paper
mill. Where his dad worked.

Where his grandfather worked.
His great grandfather.

No cycle is ever meant to
be a clean break.

Now, he watches his boy, shooting
hoops in the schoolyard where ambition
once soared…

Notices he's a bit dangly…
A little off kilter, IEP's
say he has a severe learning
disorder.

Pop looks down at the gravel
for a minute, then takes a
quick peek.

Sees his son's shot miss
the rim entirely.

Air ball.

His eyes trail back to the ground.
Squints.
Emotions fall aloof ---

Realizing, his pride and joy
isn't going
anywhere.

One more glance into
oblivion before leaving the courts.

Going slowly,
back to the migration
of nowhere.

Danny Boy and the Stone Temple Pilots

I listened to *Plush*
every day
from Nashua, New Hampshire to Hudson,
Massachusetts Hospital.

Watching my mother slowly
die from dementia.

Obviously, it a hard
witness—saying "hi"
to her while she was
screaming at some nurse
to let her go home…

She had forgotten where
home was.

Often, mom could not remember who I
was, or on the rare occasion she would recognize me,
she would call me an asshole
and tell me to leave.

You always try not to take
it personally…

Mom is sick, I understood.

So, most of my visits were short,
ten minutes at most.

Leaving to the curse words of this
beautiful Irish woman who
would sing *Danny Boy* to
me when I was a child.

I would take a quick
peek at her window
once I walked out
the exit…

Tears running down my
cheeks…

Rushing to my car
putting the keys in the
ignition as fast as I could…

Then squeal the hell out
of there—cranking more
Stone Temple Pilots…

I did not own any CD that
featured a crooner singing
Danny Boy at the time.

When she died, I still didn't have one.
and if you ask me today…I'll give
you the same lonely answer…

Arranged

I am not needed
to decipher a memoir.

Nor do I have to
tell my tale of
disgust and disdain
in an attempted fashionable
                wordplay.

I hate Pollack.
I hate disarray.

Because I have lived
that lie for 58 years.

Buck the system?
Damn, why?

Just sit—hands folded
in lap… and
watch "it" destroy itself.

No more will I be
ashamed of being a coward…

Cheryl Galley

You were the
girl who sat
in the back seat, showing
your tits to confused,
horny 13-14-year-old guys
at 6 PM—while we
were going home on the late bus.

The winter darkness contributed to
mysterious sexual excursions we
all wanted to feel.

Letting Jim Clanksdale unbutton your
shirt…

He was having the eighth grade
fun.

As the hooks of your bra were
being undone…

Only the "cool" were lucky
enough to experience this floor show.

I was sitting in the front,
adjusting my fat.

Not popular enough to
be one of the crowd.

Straining my neck.

Trying to see some real boob
for the first time in my life.

Nowhere near the three or
four boys who made a circle
around the erection exhibition…

Suddenly, the driver
flashed on the lights

"What the hell is going
on back there?" …Fat Mamma
enforcer screamed.

Hunger rushed away…Cheryl slumped down,
trying to cover up.

Boners still strict and
at embarrassing attention.

The boys turn forward—ashamed,
but truthful in their lust…

Thinking of the infield fly rule
or grandma coming out of
the shower…

To calm our libido before we
had to leave.

Trek up the hill and
go home…to the
hamburger helper, teasing older
brother…and having to take out
the
trash…

Freshman Year in College

As she was glancing through my
words—the buxom English
Professor provided a first criticism.

"You use too many double negatives",
she claimed.

Her blond hair gleaming love
letters throughout Creative Writing
101.

I blankly looked up at her,
trying to avoid staring at her tits

and said…

"I am a double negative."

She gave me a sad glance,
then moved on to the next student.

Imaginary Ideas with Everette

> *Nothing on the page is true,*
> *Only the failure...*
>   -Everette Maddox

Fixed—
In imaginary translation...

No one alive can claim
the stones are misfits
of road...

Only a lone witness,
can describe spasms of
loss

efficiently—now and then.

I have often come to
the conclusion that
my misconceptions are
laughed at by toadies...

Bards, who exist for worship
of benevolent jottings...

Praise, regrettably, will
uplift a tainted soul sometimes...

Concealing truth is the
hardest vice to surrender…
Maybe its paranoia…
Maybe its pain…

Maybe, Everette, it was all
just a lie.

Wellbutrin Blues

When the will cannot find a way
to converse with all the budding
failures of woman who are waiting
for the 4 PM bus.

I will retreat into my shell of gazing
incoherently.

Blaming the new medication I am
on for chronic depression.

Finding mental murder without
actually hurting anyone.

Behind Blood-Shot Eyes

Purity is not a trait that compounds itself
with the seedy side of town—

Especially when your stare catches the eye
of a woman with questionable morals.

And as you look down in shame, trying to disassociate
yourself with the business like gleam the streetwalker flashed
back at you moments earlier.

You wonder how many peeks a day it takes
Miss Sally Hooker to drum up some
horny cliental.

Then you question what exact day it was when
innocence left Sally's persona.

I Love That Song

Hanging around
downtown…could
care less who was lounging
in my chair…

I am not a motto
to be quoted in some
stagnant alley…

Sometimes, just too much
caffeine makes me sing to the
malcontents who carry their
wisdom through the flag
they are waving today…

Out of tune, out of touch--
Out of mind…

My song is heard—considered.
Then thrown away like a used
lottery ticket.

Going to Look for the Big Time

Little cherub
over golden
    terrain…

She never dared to
dirty a part
of her soul.

Church chimes
ring in the small
town.

Final security, that is
now thousands
of miles away.

Greyhound buses
sometimes will
empty the pockets
of chancel beauty…

Days put between
naïve virtue.

Heading towards filthy
    charm…

Searching for a dream
within a demon's lair.

Have no clue of the ending?

Rape…
Murder…
The age-old story.

Aspirations are always simple.

Reality always ends up deceased.

Stoned at Fenway

Game 162 at
Fenway…1997

Boston, 20 games out
of first place

Mo Vaughn swinging
for the fences

and swinging for a new contract
he never received.

The 3000 fans that bothered to
show up knew that
this might be the last
time seeing him in
a Red Sox Uniform.

Platt and I are sitting
in the last row of the
right field bleachers…

Smoking character—tying to
figure out how they'll be in 1998.

Asking Rudy Pemberton if he would
like a hit…

Mo strikes out in the bottom of the eight.

One more toke from the joint in honor
of the Hit Dog's last at bat.

As we leave to go to
The Cask and Flagon, Platt sums
up the whole day in four words.

"He's no Ted Williams."

Mourning

They still come
every year
carrying candles
to the graveyard.

Honoring the dead
relative…who was tragically
killed…

In some perverted way.

Where is this happening?
Does it matter?

I'll let you decide.

Two Lives in an Instant (Why I am a Moral Pussy)

He walks, arms folded across
bony chest cavity. Green neon
shirt hiding insults from long past.

Frail blue tie blowing in the wind.

Wearing light red pants, waist going
halfway to his chin. Chuck Taylor sneakers
that trip over themselves as he avoids the
tanned brunettes and bleached blond boys,
Those college fashion statements who rather
be seen and adored than focus on an education.

Standing isolated within budding cliques who
ridicule, tease and belittle the kid; he retreats
into a treasure of his own forlorn.

As I walk past him; and see the sadness he is
trying so hard to hide--He quickly stares back
at me, then looks down at the sidewalk for
some kind of moral support.

Two pony-tailed girls with white
halter-tops continue to giggle. One
cock-rock boy with a LeBron James
muscle shirt and knee-length checkered

shorts talks on his cell phone, ignoring
the lad with the strange clothes and
welling eyes.

I stop for a moment, then let him pass…he
is now two feet behind me and---*oh god,*
I should say something.

Even an acknowledgement of existence—a
hi or hello would be some source of inner light.

But I am a coward, wrapped up in my own playground
creation of torrid tears.

I say nothing to him-and he walks away…

His story still his own.
Me, less pure and more tainted.

Because some tales must remain hidden.
For all never to see.
Ever.

But once in a while, life's sacred secrets are unfortunately
witnessed…
and felt by many.

Even if you do not want them to be…

The Quiet Demeanor

Pause,
Silence—

wants to resurrect its
demons.

Wants to come back
into play.

Expressing time on a tubular
sidewalk.

Friends, enemies
stroll through your psyche with
young, unforced
insincerity.

Pause,
Silence—

Words let go.
Heard, but not comprehended.

Stop, stray.

Count steps walking
away from home.

Mouth wired shut,
no scars appear.

No jargon to diffuse.

Just,
pause,
silence—

Never to be redeemed
or heard.

In this lifetime…

Fake News Letterman List… Ten Jobs Donny Trump Can Apply for After he Leaves the Oval Office

1.) Polygrip spokesman.
2.) Writer of New Match Game "Boob jokes."
3.) Wino
4.) New celebrity info ad star for "Penis Extends."
5.) You tuber, showing "forearm workout"
6.) Lead role in new Dirty Harry movie— "Movement of Flab"
7.) Creates new soup, "Cream of Lard."
8.) Replaces Dan Aykroyd in SNL new version of Plumber buttcrack skit
9.) Fights Hillbilly Jim on WWE next pay for view… Battle for the Geritol championship.
10.) Poses nude for "Playpen" magazine…Home of the new "Whoppers."

Thesis Project

Subject for future study
by winos.

Forget about begging
for bucks when I'm already
half in the bag.

All you'll get is bumbling
philosophical dribble.

From an asshole
who thinks he has all
the answers

About everything that
is misunderstood.

Simple as That

Son, looking at the world
with unique glasses—

Writing down all
your faithful observations

inside the trusty notepad…

Get published, believe you're
an exclusive event.

Then think…the world is
looking at *you?*

That's just plain

wrong.

Family Tree

Paris Vassall was sold
to the highest bidder
for breeding purposes
at age twelve.

Four hundred years
later, your identity has
been discovered by
African American relatives.

Conversations about this fact
often has an angry, disbelief
taint.

I guess *all men were not created
equal...*

Do not turn the page.

NOTE: The above poem is a true story. Thanks to John Platt Jr. and his mother Roberta Platt for finding out this information via research.

The Place

The Lounge,
Bar, Tavern, Inn…

The place.

Where worries are beheaded…

And promises go home--

Never kept, only arranged

While fear rolls on the ground,
eyes staring up

at you during the
long stumble…

God Helps Those Who Help Themselves

Come as you are on
Sunday, 10 A.M. Even
if you're in the process
of hanging yourself—because
Monday seems impossible to face.

Northern New England is no place to
play the depressed card…

When God can still
walk you to the
lumber yard,
buy you a thermos
of coffee and
a chicken sandwich.

Tell you to say three Hail Mary's.
Then fall in love with Truth, Justice
and the only way.

The other "dribble of dankness" you can
take with you to the grave…

No one will care.

Misanthropic Suburb Wanderer

The suburban impersonal.

A quick nod of acknowledgement as
you adjust the grocery bag…

Not wanting to drop the corn chips.

The law of the land imposes that
we smile at all the imposters…

That walk in and out
        out and in…

Of our daily jaunts to freakish
normalcy.

Participate in accepted lies
when we grin at the neighbors
eating in their front yard.

You hate to say hello…

Wave.

Smile.

At Mr. Jack and Mrs. Jane drinking a beer…

Adjusting the grill…

Snot nosed little Jerry and
future prom queen Jenny run around
their parents…screaming and
hitting each other with water bombs.

Waiting for a damned frankfurter…

Must this façade continue?

Expose the cretin niceness
For all to see?

I rather study my own
despondency—

Explore the habit of
covering my face when the
threat of suburbia becomes
predictable.

Stumble over the same
bush as I walk into the
apartment building.

Break the wine bottle, drop the
bologna as I enter

another concede.

Out of the Loop

Those guys
who read *Nausea*

thinking they're cool

without a hint of irony.

Didn't know Carlson McCullers
was a girl

till five years ago.

The loop is so strenuous.

All of those wanting to get in…

Not knowing that getting out
is layered with

a pinch of
original thought.

I'm a lone confessor
In a gallowed world.

After Reading *Her*

Her boorish/ slutty charm
wore on me a bit.

Being labeled as the "coolest"
girl on the block—

Did not enhance words of
old Bukowski wisdom.

Sharing items of fucked-up
relationships so bluntly,

then walking away with
some transcendent dignity maybe
works on a hobby horse who pales as
a steed.

But constantly describing
yourself as the misguided
observer often
lacks innovation…

Benatar already told us *love is a
battlefield*—you are not unique
in confessing that many of your
desired, perplexed lines are just futile
heartbreak cannon fodder.

There have been many who've tried
to drink each other off their minds…

Ask Mick Jagger…

So, yea—your poesy now
sits on my bookshelf, along with
the other champs, chumps, and clowns
who classify themselves as poets…

Being slotted as the user/abuser
can sometimes dress an old man down

Searching for Real

For Mike Taylor

I've chased the gods
many times in

dreaded dreams
where I was hoping to touch
at least a tassel of a robe or

find a hint of *something that
truly exists.*

Sometimes, I also feel a touch
on my shoulder during a 37 Miller Lite
binge.

…A ghost that
whispers in my ear,

Saying--

And even if you could, so what?

I raise my bottle…
Toasting the invisible,
quiet hero…

Hoping he could

hop the gate around
my fence

…and tell me

if I should or not?

Mike Webster

You would think
the NFL would initiate
a holiday for old
piano arms…

Pulling on a screen pass…

Taking out pursuit by
leading with his head.

Knocking down
potential tacklers

As Franco or Rocky
scooted into the endzone.

Triceps bulging as he went back
to the huddle…
Ready for some more
helmet to helmet
contact…

It is just unfortunate
that he was slowly
dying while doing his
job…

A scrambled noggin
back in the day was
seen as a badge
of courage
for lineman…

Could care less that
too many times, your
brain would slosh to the other
side of your skull…

During the millions
of collisions that
took place

during practice
and games…

But god damn it,
Bless Mike Webster…

He gave so much to
the Steelers dynasty…

Play after play, year
after year…

Not knowing
while in the process.

He gave the ultimate
sacrifice.

Give Up

Late concede.

I fell…between
thought and pictures
of forever's past…

I lost so many
battles—inner finalities
led me to the bloody cross…

Shamed for crimes
I did not commit.

Walk the eternal circle
with me…

Please.

Way Too Late

And at all the
high points
of craziness…

Huey, Selby,
Kaufman

All the morbid sane
who spurned their
chance at normalcy…

With a thimble
      parade

of one…

Preaching to the silhouette
choir…
    Following.
Not following

mirth in the end.

Candidates that
      sparkled
      faded…

Walked away
on phantom's terms.

Not Me

Maybe, that what genius does to some.
It gives them a borderline where greatness is so excessive that
the chosen few teeter on the brink of insanity…
Then, suddenly…it's gone, left with
a comedown of mental lonesome…
And you can be in the middle of the mouth
of madness without leaving the couch…

Detachment

So, what happened to you?
Always the question
for those who think
      you're crazy…

Some days are just filled
with limited space.

86'ed

Barred from Wonderland
with an idea of poetic license
stuck to my calamity.

Billowing hopelessness stalks the
ground with the horizontal
homeless.

Before I go, I'll take three of what she's
having and call it a life.

Be patient, as I count the
pennies to pay the tab.

You've got nowhere to
go Captain America…

Being 86'ed forever is a
title I'd welcome
      warmly…

I can sit on the curb
all day now

and portray my pitiful
mistake.

As passer byes lean against my
new home.

Trying to lift gum off
their shoe.

Confessions of Mourning

You decipher pain and sorrow while watching stragglers walk up and down the street through your filthy window. Another testimonial of simple motor skill seems absurd, like lifeless cattle on the side of the road,

                    the dead humanity that wipes away the crust from the side of his/her mouth.

Don't we all want serenity for the cheapest price?

A weekly visit to the holy shrine in the middle of your town— knee benders worship secretion from other morally catatonic erasures. Filling their need for meat from the souls of those

                who truly mourn the departure?

Isn't grief convenient?

Thoughts can attempt to defuse time; faith will get you a paycheck plus a good night sleep.

You see carpe diem is useless. Days only blend into other ludicrous adventures. The descriptions of routine is depressing enough, never is there mention of shade.

Shade, we'll all be covered in it shortly.

Jesus, an accepted carcass, placing bets, weekends—bear no witness to a terminal diagnosis.

I have little energy left to bathe in disgust.

And time is not precious to me.

Rent your port of emotions on a dirty sleeve.

After being gone for a short time, the pain for those left behind will become less and less.

An afterthought of a stroll we do not understand.

Our love avoiding the inevitable will one day face the flames.

All the morbid tricks and treats we gave to ourselves, pushing it one

more year—

One more month.

Collapses.

The man, who is half frozen,

dead, still--

Has lied on Route 16 for two weeks.

Rotting…

Ignored…

While the rest of the clan

regenerate, relax.

Skim through a photo album
of Christmas memories.

Seeming so bland--

Going through the motions…

As more and more disappear into
an island
of end.

Give me no more tangent feedback concerning tragic belief.

The struggle is so far away, but as close as the nearest calendar.

My maturity level—

Never was considered
for any sort of

durable goods.

Waiting for the Cardiologist

My confessions are
made of gold.

No will of the wisp
Friday walk through--

Trying to find cheap heaven.

Beatings have terrorized
the old ticker; many self-inflicted.

But as I dream of gurneys
wheeling my fat carcass into
some death & destruction room.

I refuse to mask my evil secrets.
Even as I am entrenched into
the cold
dark terrain.

Trying Nature Out

There it is—driving
around northern New Hampshire.

Trying to find a lost paradise within
these god damned dark woods…

December two thousand and something.

Slim pickings in the forest today.

No deer, or moose,
not even a squirrel collecting acorns.

Just the same emptiness your father
never told you about.

Thought nature could possibly nurture,
help elect a symptom
for me to finally contort
into inner peace.

Na, just another day…
Not happening.

Self-Interviews
never turn out well
when you're cruising
from nowhere to here.

It's just another failed
attempt.

The hope of god's
creations, to fill your
torture

with hope.

But, you pull
over—turn the car around
and head home.

Enter the driveway, consider
other possibilities,

you might
try
tomorrow…

Pure and Hard

The whole hooded
poet, philosopher
bit—

Ain't working.

So, I will try to compress the truth.

We all die.

Help *me* dealt with *it*.

Never Could Figure Out

To those 90's all-terrain
bands who tried to touch
an evil/soft spot in my
already frozen psyche…

You lost me out of the gate.
I could never understand what you
Were saying

and

I was too busy, checking out
the size of my triceps, amid hazy,
gauzy mirrors behind some neutral
bartender-- who could care less

of my Who fetish, which I
fulfilled piling dollar bills into
some aged
     juke which would
never deny me "Quadrophenia."

A former collegiate offensive lineman and football coach for 26 years, Dan Provost's poetry has been published both online and in print since 1995. He is the author of thirteen books/chapbooks. His latest, December 22, 2020 *Playing Croquet in Short Pants During a Snowstorm,* was recently published by Alien Buddha Press. He has been nominated for the Best of the Net and has read his work throughout the United States. He lives in Berlin, New Hampshire with his wife Laura, and dog Bella.